Usborne Sticker
Atlas
of the
World

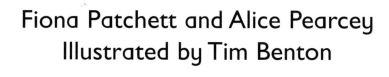

Fiona Patchett and Alice Pearcey
Illustrated by Tim Benton

Designed by Sarah Cronin,
Stephen Moncrieff and Lucy Owen

Edited by Gillian Doherty
Consultant: Zoë Tomlinson

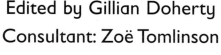

Contents

ARCTIC OCEAN

North and Central America

Europe

The Middle East

ATLANTIC OCEAN

Africa

PACIFIC OCEAN

South America

Antarctica

Asia

PACIFIC
OCEAN

INDIAN
OCEAN

Australasia

How to use this book

There are more than 140 stickers in this book, showing some of the most famous sights in the world, including the Great Wall of China and Niagara Falls. To find out where each one is, try to match the stickers in the middle of the book to the black and white drawings on the maps.

The stickers are numbered, so you can tell which map they go on. A list on each map tells you the names of the sights, and there's a checklist at the back of the book to help you.

Using the maps

The shading on the maps on pages 4–15 shows what the land is like in different places. This key explains what the shading and the lines on the maps represent.

▇ Forests	▇ Seas and oceans
▇ Deserts	▢ Lakes
▇ Mountains	∫ Rivers
▢ Tundra	∫ Country boundaries
▢ Ice and snow	⌐ Country boundaries through water
▢ Other (grassland, farmland and cities)	

World maps

Every map in this book has a small world map next to it. The area shaded red shows you which part of the world is shown on the big map.

This is the world map that goes with the big map of South America on pages 10–11.

Africa

Mediterranean Sea

MOROCCO

Madeira (Portugal)

TUNISIA

Canary Islands (Spain)

ALGERIA

LIBYA

WESTERN SAHARA (Morocco)

MALI

MAURITANIA

NIGER

CH

CAPE VERDE

SENEGAL

THE GAMBIA

BURKINA FASO

GUINEA-BISSAU

GUINEA

GHANA

BENIN

TOGO

NIGERIA

SIERRA LEONE

IVORY COAST

LIBERIA

ATLANTIC OCEAN

CAMEROON

EQUATORIAL GUINEA

SAO TOME AND PRINCIPE

GABON

CONGO

ANGOL

NAM

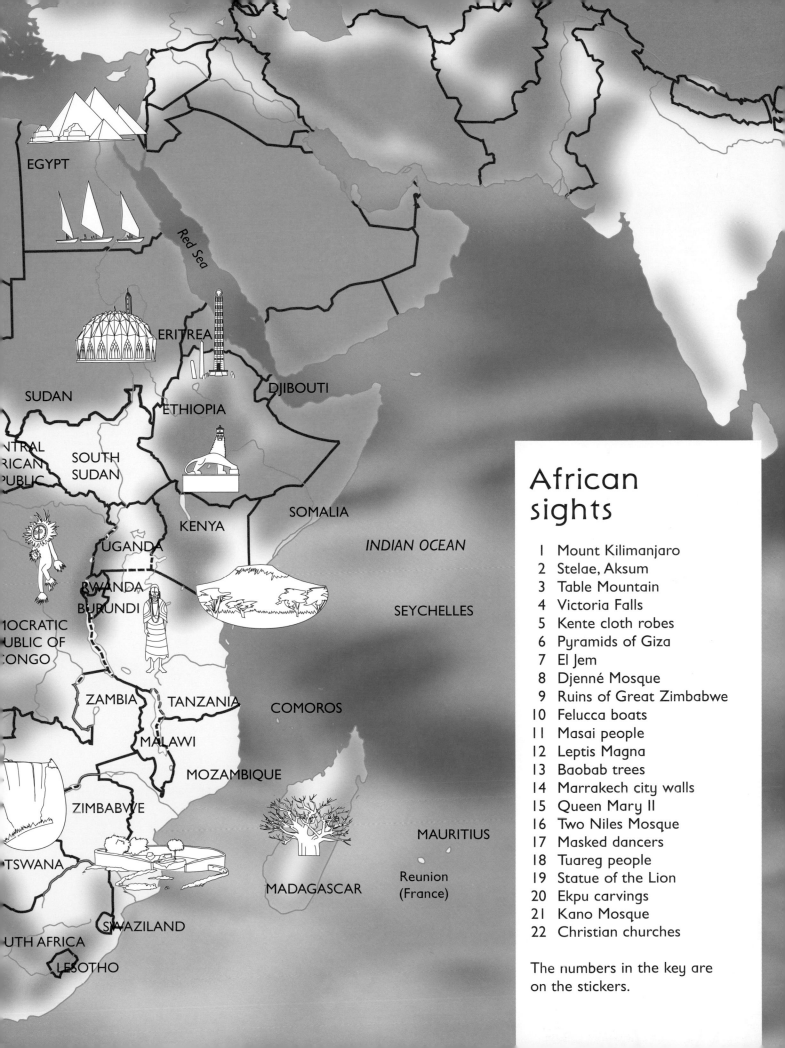

EGYPT

Red Sea

ERITREA

SUDAN

DJIBOUTI

ETHIOPIA

NTRAL
RICAN
PUBLIC

SOUTH
SUDAN

SOMALIA

KENYA

UGANDA

INDIAN OCEAN

RWANDA
BURUNDI

MOCRATIC
UBLIC OF
ONGO

SEYCHELLES

ZAMBIA

TANZANIA

COMOROS

MALAWI

MOZAMBIQUE

ZIMBABWE

MAURITIUS

TSWANA

Reunion
(France)

MADAGASCAR

SWAZILAND

UTH AFRICA

LESOTHO

African sights

1   Mount Kilimanjaro
2   Stelae, Aksum
3   Table Mountain
4   Victoria Falls
5   Kente cloth robes
6   Pyramids of Giza
7   El Jem
8   Djenné Mosque
9   Ruins of Great Zimbabwe
10 Felucca boats
11 Masai people
12 Leptis Magna
13 Baobab trees
14 Marrakech city walls
15 Queen Mary II
16 Two Niles Mosque
17 Masked dancers
18 Tuareg people
19 Statue of the Lion
20 Ekpu carvings
21 Kano Mosque
22 Christian churches

The numbers in the key are
on the stickers.

Asia

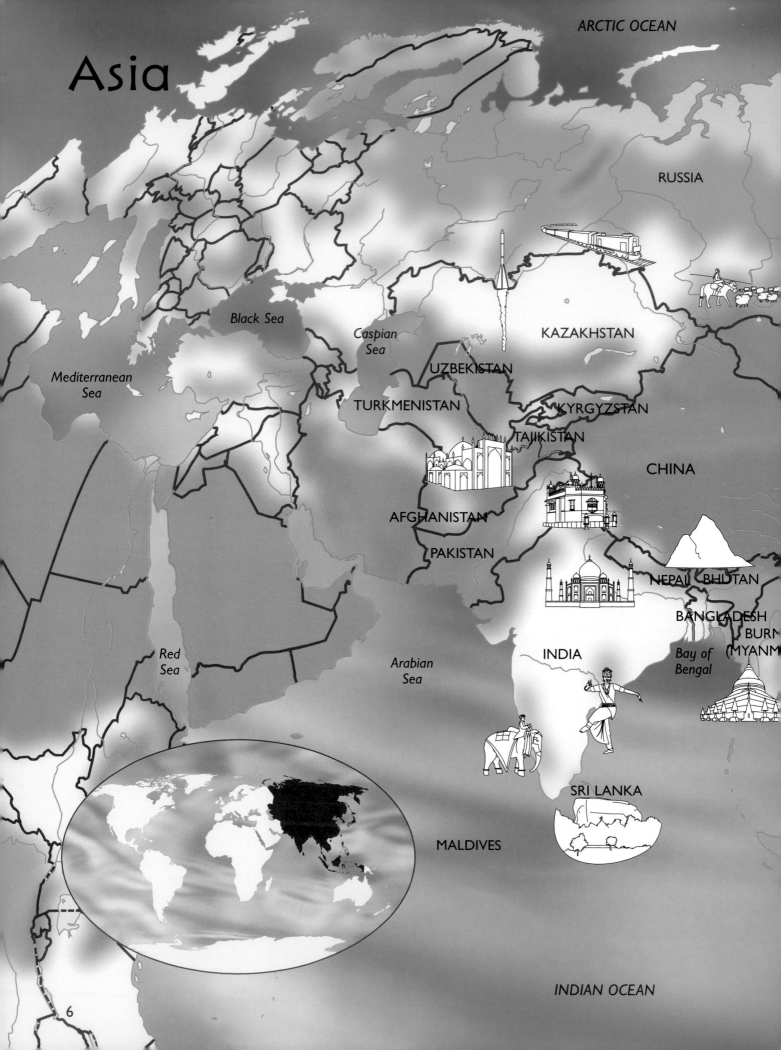

ARCTIC OCEAN

RUSSIA

KAZAKHSTAN

Black Sea

Caspian
Sea

UZBEKISTAN

TURKMENISTAN

KYRGYZSTAN

TAJIKISTAN

Mediterranean
Sea

CHINA

AFGHANISTAN

PAKISTAN

NEPAL BHUTAN

BANGLADESH

BURM

MYANM

Red
Sea

Arabian
Sea

INDIA

Bay of
Bengal

SRI LANKA

MALDIVES

INDIAN OCEAN

Asian sights

The numbers in the key are
on the stickers.

Bering Sea

Sea of Okhotsk

Sea of Japan

NGOLIA

NORTH KOREA

SOUTH KOREA

JAPAN

Taiwan

VIETNAM

OS

South China Sea

ILAND

MBODIA

PHILIPPINES

Philippine Sea

PACIFIC OCEAN

BRUNEI

AYSIA

GAPORE

Borneo

Celebes

umatra

INDONESIA

New Guinea

Java

EAST TIMOR

7

North and Central America

ATLANTIC
OCEAN

Newfoundland

GREENLAND
(Denmark)

Labrador
Sea

Baffin
Bay

Ellesmere
Island

Baffin
Island

Queen Elizabeth
Islands

Hudson
Bay

Victoria
Island

ARCTIC OCEAN

Beaufort
Sea

CANADA

ALASKA (USA)

Gulf of
Alaska

PACIFIC
OCEAN

North and Central American sights

47 Grand Canyon
48 Niagara Falls
49 Day of the Dead festival
50 Mount McKinley
51 Mississippi paddle boats
52 Giant redwood trees
53 CN Tower
54 Panama Canal
55 Totem poles
56 Pueblo de Taos
57 Statue of Liberty
58 Kennedy Space Center
59 Mount Rushmore
60 Chichen Itza
61 Hollywood
62 Gateway Arch
63 Seattle Space Needle
64 Calgary stampede
65 Old Havana Cathedral
66 White House
67 Inuit people
68 Mayan temple, Tikal
69 Golden Gate Bridge
70 Ice hockey players

The numbers in the key are on the stickers.

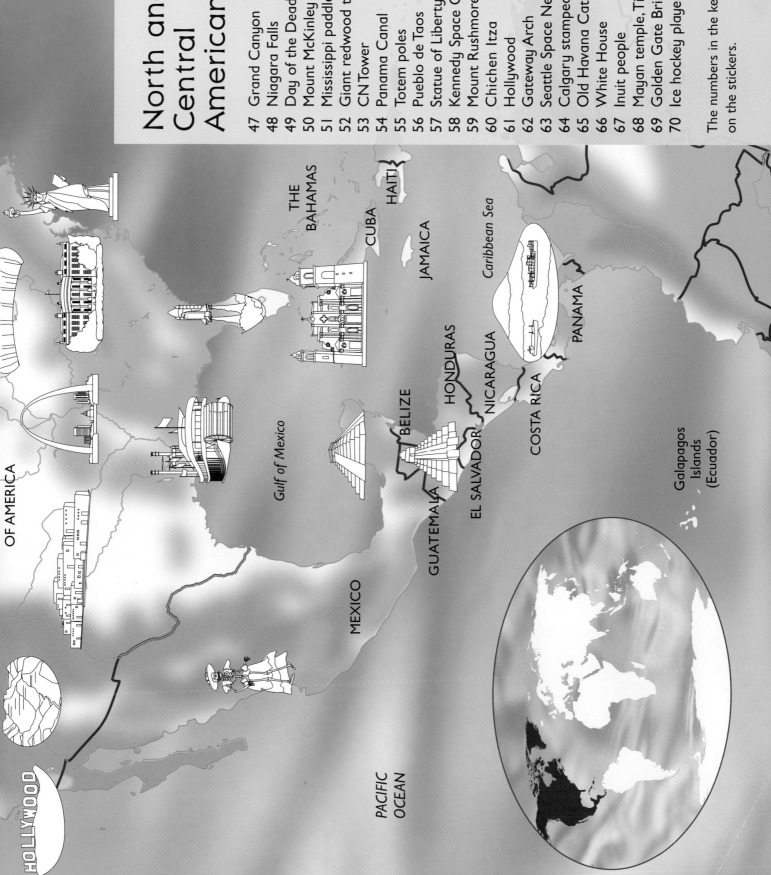

HOLLYWOOD

PACIFIC OCEAN

OF AMERICA

Gulf of Mexico

MEXICO

THE BAHAMAS

CUBA

HAITI

JAMAICA

BELIZE

GUATEMALA

HONDURAS

EL SALVADOR

NICARAGUA

COSTA RICA

Caribbean Sea

PANAMA

Galapagos Islands (Ecuador)

South America

Caribbean Sea

ATLANTIC OCEAN

VENEZUELA

GUYANA

SURINAME

FRENCH GUIANA (France)

COLOMBIA

ECUADOR

PERU

BRAZIL

BOLIVIA

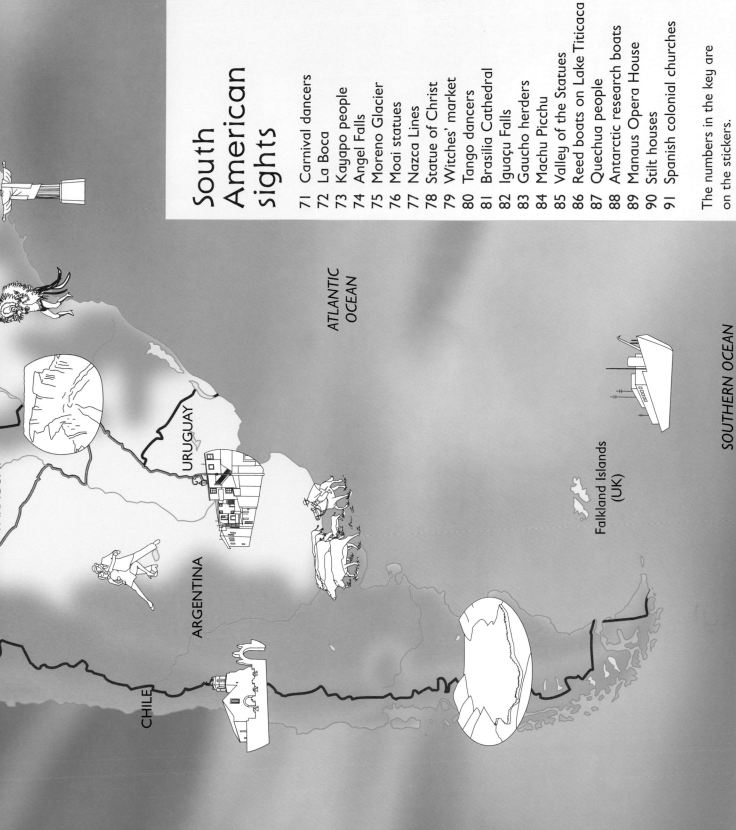

South American sights

71 Carnival dancers
72 La Boca
73 Kayapo people
74 Angel Falls
75 Moreno Glacier
76 Moai statues
77 Nazca Lines
78 Statue of Christ
79 Witches' market
80 Tango dancers
81 Brasilia Cathedral
82 Iguaçu Falls
83 Gaucho herders
84 Machu Picchu
85 Valley of the Statues
86 Reed boats on Lake Titicaca
87 Quechua people
88 Antarctic research boats
89 Manaus Opera House
90 Stilt houses
91 Spanish colonial churches

The numbers in the key are on the stickers.

ATLANTIC OCEAN

URUGUAY

ARGENTINA

CHILE

Falkland Islands (UK)

SOUTHERN OCEAN

PACIFIC OCEAN

Easter Island is 2,300 miles (3,700 km) from the coast of Chile.

The Middle East

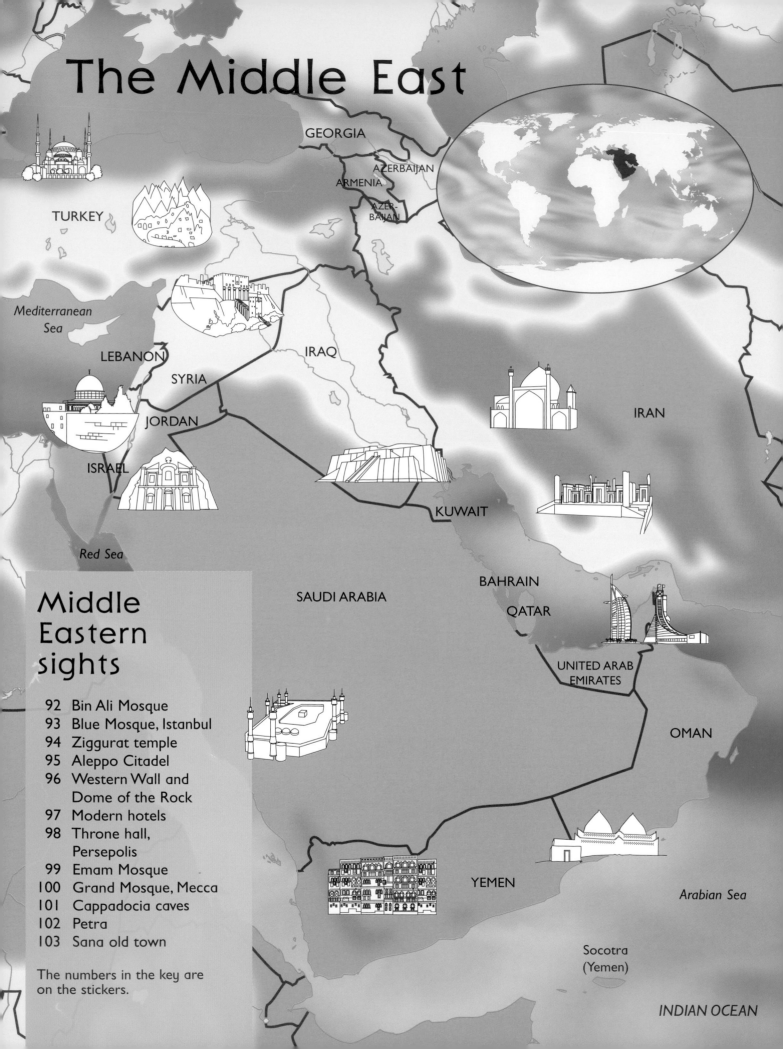

GEORGIA

AZERBAIJAN

ARMENIA

AZER-
BAIJAN

TURKEY

Mediterranean
Sea

IRAQ

LEBANON

SYRIA

JORDAN

IRAN

ISRAEL

Red Sea

KUWAIT

BAHRAIN

SAUDI ARABIA

QATAR

UNITED ARAB
EMIRATES

OMAN

YEMEN

Arabian Sea

Socotra
(Yemen)

INDIAN OCEAN

Middle Eastern sights

The numbers in the key are
on the stickers.

 58

 30

 42

 20

 139

 125

 91

 107

 43

 52

 106

 67

 73

 121

 109

 45

 130

 40

 115

 16

 76

 105

 88

 68

 5

 80

 86

 46

 118

 95

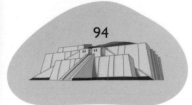 94

 128

 13

 137

 61

HOLLYWOOD

 104

 135

 49

 83

 77

 143

 38

 11

 23

 15

 1

 96

 62

 113

 92

 85

 27

 97

 84

 54

 63

 26

 141

 6

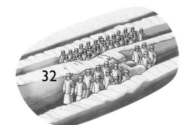 32

 120

 18

 98

 66

 14

 112

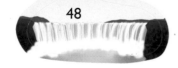 48

 138

 87

 55

 100

 8

 51

 39

 50

 126

 103

 114

 74

 57

 136

 10

 134

 117

 34

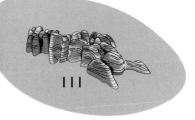 90

 41

 21

 99

 111

 119

 12

 44

 7

89

 24

 29

 69

 140

 3

 129

 33

 47

 133

 101

 142

 4

 28

 78

 65

 144

 9

 81

 31

 124

93

 59

 102

 79

 22

 53

 64

 19

 108

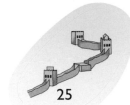 25

 132

 37

 56

 82

 75

 17

 122

 127

 131

 116

 36

 70

 71

 123

 110

 72

2

35

60

Australasia

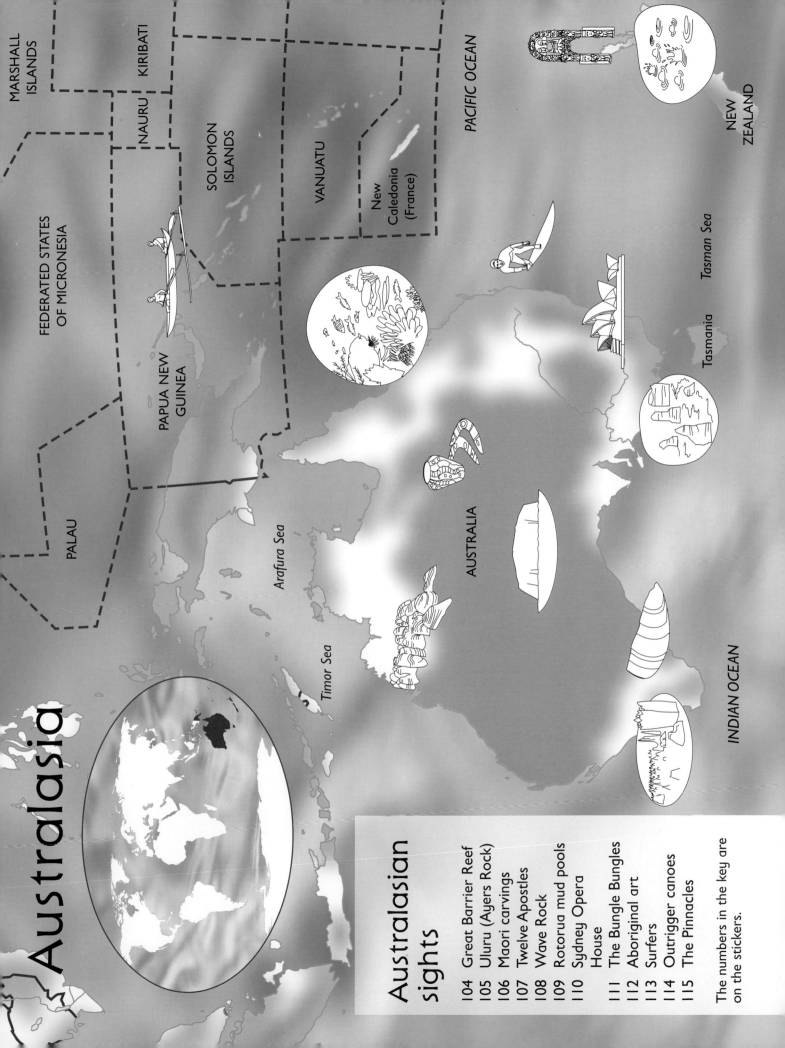

MARSHALL ISLANDS

NAURU

KIRIBATI

SOLOMON ISLANDS

VANUATU

New Caledonia (France)

PACIFIC OCEAN

NEW ZEALAND

FEDERATED STATES OF MICRONESIA

PAPUA NEW GUINEA

PALAU

Arafura Sea

Timor Sea

AUSTRALIA

Tasmania

Tasman Sea

INDIAN OCEAN

Australasian sights

104 Great Barrier Reef
105 Uluru (Ayers Rock)
106 Maori carvings
107 Twelve Apostles
108 Wave Rock
109 Rotorua mud pools
110 Sydney Opera House
111 The Bungle Bungles
112 Aboriginal art
113 Surfers
114 Outrigger canoes
115 The Pinnacles

The numbers in the key are on the stickers.

Europe

ICELAND

ARCTIC OCEAN

Norwegian Sea

NORWAY

SWE

North
Sea

DENMARK

IRELAND

UNITED
KINGDOM

ATLANTIC OCEAN

NETHERLANDS

BELGIUM   GERMANY

LUX.*

CZEC
REPUB

AUSTR

Bay of Biscay

FRANCE   SWITZERLAND

SLOVEN

CROA

SAN
MARINO

ITALY

Corsica

PORTUGAL

SPAIN

Sardinia

Mediterranean Sea

Sicily

MALTA

14

Barents Sea

FINLAND

RUSSIA

ESTONIA

LATVIA

Baltic Sea

LITHUANIA

BELARUS

POLAND

UKRAINE

SLOVAKIA

MOLDOVA

HUNGARY

ROMANIA

SERBIA

Black Sea

BULGARIA

KOSOVO

MONTE-GRO

MACEDONIA

TURKEY

ALBANIA

GREECE

Aegean Sea

CYPRUS

Crete

European sights

116 Ballet dancers
117 Strokkur geyser
118 Olavinlinna Castle
119 Giant's Causeway
120 Bran Castle
121 Belem Tower
122 Ice hotel
123 Neuschwanstein Castle
124 St. Basil's Cathedral
125 The Colosseum
126 Wooden churches
127 Eiffel Tower
128 Palace of Westminster
129 Celtic crosses
130 The Little Mermaid
131 Church of the
    Sagrada Familia
132 The Parthenon
133 Malbork Castle
134 Mount Etna
135 Winter Palace
136 Mont St. Michel
137 Tyn Church
138 Sami people
139 Leaning Tower of Pisa
140 Guggenheim Museum,
    Bilbao
141 Edinburgh Castle
142 Flamenco dancers
143 Cossack dancers
144 Minoan palace

The numbers in the key are
on the stickers.

*LUX. = LUXEMBOURG

Flags of the world

These pages show the flags of the world's 195 independent states. The name of the state and its capital city are given below each flag.

Africa

Morocco
Rabat

Algeria
Algiers

Tunisia
Tunis

Libya
Tripoli

Egypt
Cairo

Mauritania
Nouakchott

Mali
Bamako

Niger
Niamey

Chad
N'Djamena

Sudan
Khartoum

South Sudan
Juba

Eritrea
Asmara

Ethiopia
Addis Ababa

Djibouti
Djibouti

Somalia
Mogadishu

Cape Verde
Praia

Senegal
Dakar

The Gambia
Banjul

Guinea-Bissau
Bissau

Guinea
Conakry

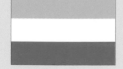
Sierra Leone
Freetown

Liberia
Monrovia

Ivory Coast
Yamoussoukro

Burkina Faso
Ouagadougou

Ghana
Accra

Togo
Lome

Benin
Porto-Novo

Nigeria
Abuja

Cameroon
Yaounde

Central African Republic
Bangui

Equatorial Guinea
Malabo

Sao Tome and Principe
Sao Tome

Gabon
Libreville

Congo
Brazzaville

Democratic Republic of the Congo
Kinshasa

Uganda
Kampala

Kenya
Nairobi

Seychelles
Victoria

Rwanda
Kigali

Burundi
Bujumbura

Tanzania
Dar es Salaam, Dodoma

Angola
Luanda

Zambia
Lusaka

Malawi
Lilongwe

Mozambique
Maputo

Zimbabwe
Harare

Comoros
Moroni

Madagascar
Antananarivo

Mauritius
Port Louis

Namibia
Windhoek

Botswana
Gaborone

South Africa
Pretoria, Cape Town, Bloemfontein

Lesotho
Maseru

Swaziland
Mbabane, Lobamba

Asia

Russia
Moscow

Georgia
Tbilisi

Armenia
Yerevan

Azerbaijan
Baku

Kazakhstan
Astana

Uzbekistan
Tashkent

Turkmenistan
Ashgabat (Ashkhabad)

Tajikistan
Dushanbe

Kyrgyzstan
Bishkek

China
Beijing

Asia (continued)

Mongolia
Ulan Bator

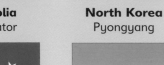

North Korea
Pyongyang

South Korea
Seoul

Japan
Tokyo

Afghanistan
Kabul

Pakistan
Islamabad

India
New Delhi

Nepal
Kathmandu

Bhutan
Thimphu

Bangladesh
Dhaka

Burma (Myanmar)
Rangoon, Nay Pyi Taw

Thailand
Bangkok

Laos
Vientiane

Cambodia
Phnom Penh

Vietnam
Hanoi

Philippines
Manila

Maldives
Male

Sri Lanka
Colombo, Sri
Jayewardenepura Kotte

Malaysia
Kuala Lumpur

Singapore
Singapore

Brunei
Bandar Seri Begawan

Indonesia
Jakarta

East Timor
Dili

North and Central America

Canada
Ottawa

**United States
of America**
Washington D.C.

Mexico
Mexico City

Guatemala
Guatemala City

Belize
Belmopan

El Salvador
San Salvador

Honduras
Tegucigalpa

Nicaragua
Managua

Costa Rica
San Jose

Panama
Panama City

North and Central America (continued)

The Bahamas
Nassau

Cuba
Havana

Jamaica
Kingston

Haiti
Port-au-Prince

Dominican Republic
Santo Domingo

Saint Kitts and Nevis
Basseterre

Antigua and Barbuda
Saint John's

Dominica
Roseau

Saint Lucia
Castries

Saint Vincent and the Grenadines
Kingstown

Barbados
Bridgetown

Grenada
Saint George's

Trinidad and Tobago
Port-of-Spain

South America

Colombia
Bogota

Venezuela
Caracas

Guyana
Georgetown

Suriname
Paramaribo

Ecuador
Quito

Peru
Lima

Brazil
Brasilia

Bolivia
La Paz, Sucre

Paraguay
Asuncion

Chile
Santiago

Argentina
Buenos Aires

Uruguay
Montevideo

The Middle East

Turkey
Ankara

Syria
Damascus

Iraq
Baghdad

Iran
Tehran

Lebanon
Beirut

The Middle East (continued)

Israel
Jerusalem

Jordan
Amman

Saudi Arabia
Riyadh

Kuwait
Kuwait City

Bahrain
Manama

Qatar
Doha

United Arab Emirates
Abu Dhabi

Oman
Muscat

Yemen
Sana

Australasia and Oceania

Palau
Melekeok

Federated States of Micronesia
Palikir

Marshall Islands
Majuro

Papua New Guinea
Port Moresby

Nauru
Yaren

Kiribati
Bairiki (on Tarawa island)

Solomon Islands
Honiara

Tuvalu
Funafuti

Samoa
Apia

Australia
Canberra

Vanuatu
Port Vila

Fiji
Suva

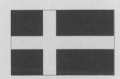
Tonga
Nukualofa

New Zealand
Wellington

Europe

Iceland
Reykjavik

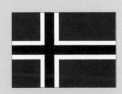
Norway
Oslo

Sweden
Stockholm

Finland
Helsinki

Ireland
Dublin

United Kingdom
London

Netherlands
Amsterdam, The Hague

Belgium
Brussels

Luxembourg
Luxembourg

Germany
Berlin

Europe (continued)

Denmark
Copenhagen

Poland
Warsaw

Lithuania
Vilnius

Latvia
Riga

Estonia
Tallinn

Belarus
Minsk

Czech Republic
Prague

Slovakia
Bratislava

Ukraine
Kiev

France
Paris

Switzerland
Bern

Liechtenstein
Vaduz

Austria
Vienna

Hungary
Budapest

Romania
Bucharest

Moldova
Chisinau

Portugal
Lisbon

Spain
Madrid

Andorra
Andorra la Vella

Monaco
Monaco

Italy
Rome

San Marino
San Marino

Vatican City
Vatican City

Slovenia
Ljubljana

Croatia
Zagreb

Bosnia and Herzegovina
Sarajevo

Serbia
Belgrade

Albania
Tirana

Macedonia
Skopje

Bulgaria
Sofia

Greece
Athens

Malta
Valletta

Cyprus
Nicosia

Montenegro
Podgorica

Kosovo
Pristina

World records

Here are some of the world's longest rivers, tallest buildings, highest mountains and other incredible world records.

The highest mountains

- Everest, Nepal/China   8,848m   (29,029ft)
- K2, Pakistan/China   8,611m   (28,251ft)
- Kanchenjunga, India/Nepal   8,586m   (28,169ft)
- Lhotse, Nepal/China   8,516m   (27,940ft)
- Makalu, Nepal/China   8,462m   (27,762ft)
- Cho Oyu, Nepal/China   8,201m   (26,906ft)
- Dhaulagiri, Nepal   8,167m   (26,795ft)
- Manaslu, Nepal   8,156m   (26,759ft)
- Nanga Parbat, Pakistan   8,126m   (26,660ft)
- Annapurna, Nepal   8,091m   (26,545ft)

Mountain ranges

The world's longest mountain range is the Andes, which stretches along the west of South America from Venezuela to the southern tip of Chile. The highest range is the Himalayas, in Asia. It has all the top ten highest mountains except K2.

Wet and dry

The Amazon Rainforest, in South America, is the wettest place in the world. The driest place is the Atacama Desert, also in South America, where it has rained only a few times in the last 400 years.

Longest rivers

- Amazon, South America   6,800km   (4,225 miles)
- Nile, Africa   6,671km   (4,145 miles)
- Chang Jiang (Yangtze), China   6,380km   (3,964 miles)
- Mississippi/Missouri, USA   6,019km   (3,740 miles)
- Yenisey/Angara, Russia   5,539km   (3,445 miles)
- Huang He (Yellow), China   5,464km   (3,398 miles)
- Ob/Irtysh/Black Irtysh, Asia   5,411km   (3,362 miles)
- Congo, Africa   4,700km   (2,920 miles)
- Lena, Russia   4,472km   (2,778 miles)
- Amur/Shilka/Onon, Asia   4,416km   (2,744 miles)

Famous waterfalls

- Angel Falls, Venezuela   979m   (3,212ft)
- Sutherland Falls, New Zealand   580m   (1,903ft)
- Mardalfossen, Norway   517m   (1,696ft)
- Jog Falls, India   253m   (830ft)
- Victoria Falls, Zimbabwe/Zambia   108m   (355ft)
- Iguaçu Falls, Brazil/Argentina   82m   (269ft)
- Niagara Falls, Canada/USA   52m   (167ft)

Naming Angel Falls

Angel Falls were discovered in 1935. They were named after James Angel, an American who crashed his plane near them in 1937.

Biggest natural lakes

- Caspian Sea   370,999 sq km   (143,244 sq miles)
- Lake Superior   82,414 sq km   (31,820 sq miles)
- Lake Victoria   69,215 sq km   (26,724 sq miles)
- Lake Huron   59,600 sq km   (23,010 sq miles)
- Lake Michigan   58,000 sq km   (22,400 sq miles)
- Lake Tanganyika   32,900 sq km   (12,702 sq miles)
- Lake Baikal   31,494 sq km   (12,160 sq miles)
- Great Bear Lake   31,153 sq km   (12,028 sq miles)
- Lake Nyasa   29,600 sq km   (11,428 sq miles)
- Great Slave Lake   28,568 sq km   (11,030 sq miles)

Deep water

The deepest lake in the world is Russia's Lake Baikal. It is 1,642m (5,387ft) deep. The deepest part of the ocean is the Pacific Ocean's Mariana Trench, whose deepest point is about 11,000m (36,090ft) deep.

Biggest islands

- Greenland   2,166,086 sq km   (836,330 sq miles)
- New Guinea   786,000 sq km   (303,476 sq miles)
- Borneo   748,168 sq km   (288,869 sq miles)
- Madagascar   587,713 sq km   (226,917 sq miles)
- Baffin Island   507,451 sq km   (195,928 sq miles)
- Sumatra   443,066 sq km   (171,069 sq miles)
- Honshu   225,800 sq km   (87,182 sq miles)
- Victoria Island   217,291 sq km   (83,897 sq miles)
- Great Britain   209,331 sq km   (80,823 sq miles)
- Ellesmere Island   196,236 sq km   (75,767 sq miles)

Big and small

The biggest country in the world is Russia, which covers an area of 17,075,200 sq km (6,592,772 sq miles). The smallest is Vatican City, which measures only 0.44 sq km (0.17 sq miles).

Tallest inhabited buildings

- Burj Khalifa, UAE   828m   (2,716ft)
- Taipei 101 Tower, Taiwan   508m   (1,677ft)
- Shanghai World Financial Center, China   492m   (1,614ft)
- International Commerce Center Hong Kong, China   484m   (1,588ft)
- Petronas Towers, Malaysia   452m   (1,483ft)
- Zifeng Tower, China   450m   (1,476ft)
- Willis (Sears) Tower, USA   442.1m   (1,450ft)
- Kingkey 100, China   441.8m   (1,449ft)
- Guangzhou International Finance Center, China   437.5m   (1,435ft)
- Trump International Hotel & Tower, USA   423.4m   (1,389ft)

Crowded places

The least populated country is Vatican City, where only around 900 people live. The most populated is China, with a population of over 1.3 billion. A third of the people in the world live in China and India.

Index and checklist

This checklist will help you to find the sights in the book. The first number after each entry tells you which page it is on. The second number is the number on the sticker.

Additional design by Kate Fearn and Neil Francis
Editorial assistance by Rachel Firth and Leonie Pratt. This edition updated by Phil Clarke.
Cartographer: Craig Asquith
Flags consultant: Jos Poels
Flag images by worldflagpictures.com